Freed

By

Words

Words are spoken to express understanding
from a point of personal perspective.
Realize that your point of perception is not able
to be perceived by anyone else,
only interpreted by your spoken word.
Describe carefully

.

We are all the center of our own universe

I just thought
That you should know
I never would of let you go
But then I blinked
And you were gone
Life just continued on
As I sat waiting
Patiently
For you to never return to me

Before I could take another breath
It was falling
Crumbling
Faster than I had ever seen something
Decay

You are wearing your trauma and that's what
makes you dangerous

Perhaps

I am confused

But so are you

With eyes that see
and
a heart that hears
my words
will you use your lips
to speak against
the injustice that
infiltrates
our worlds

Unbearable and yet you wear it well
That sour smell of anguish
Some things plain
For the eyes to see
But I need you to hear me

There are pieces of me in places
              you've never been

a sinner in soft skin

Can't seem to find the time
To find my mind
It's racing
Blazing past me
Always got me asking

I hear you
Out there
In the wind
Wondering where I've been

"Haven't been in the same room for so long."
And then you're gone

Miles
and
miles
stretched
before
wild
tired
eyes
but
she
cant
stop
running
from
herself

What if
no one else
is really here
they're all just a test
and you've been ignoring every one
so you're failing really bad
the only advice your teacher gave
was to give it all you had
so don't keep it to yourself
you've got a
world
to
grab

He couldn't bring himself to look at her,
to dare let his eyes dance across the pale skin of
her full face,
across the freckles on the bridge of her nose
and the tops of her cheeks.
Under her eyes that changed color with her
ever changing mood,
lastly, to her dark pink lips, the bottom one she
sucks on when she stares at him.
He can't look at her, he shouldn't look at her.
It will kill him to look at her.
He has someone, he is happy now.
He can't look at her
But he does.
She isn't looking at him though,
and so he looks away.
A few moments pass, and again he looks at her.
She sees him out of the corner of her eye and
looks right into him.
He sees it kills her, whole body tensing, yet she
never looks away,
she'll hold his gaze.

(continued.)

She stares right back into his eyes and he
falters every time.
Though his expression rarely changes and
never is a word said,
everything is there in his eyes, for her to see,
and she knows.
But he says nothing, so she has nothing left to
say.
She knows she shouldn't meet his eyes,
because it will break her,
but she does it everytime,
and he looks at her anyways, shows her how he
feels
because he knows he'll never tell her
and she knows.

(end.)

We're
all
just
Matter,
trying
to
matter

Sprinkle a little of your style on the world
The way you do things
Don't just sit around
Wasting time
Marinating in your blue dreams

He was an angel

meant to save her

but

he burned himself

just to lie with

her

You are going to want

more from the

world and some

people are going

to hate you

for

it

The doctors feed her pills to forget,
and she does.
She forgets that her family loves her,
that her life is worth living,
busy swimming in a xanax pool,
constant state of confused.

She used to be a stressed mother,
a good man's lover.
Now she's an empty addict,
laying on top of dirty covers.

I've grown up to realize that some doctors,
are monsters,
and
I miss my mother

Just
because

you
don't

want
to

look
at

it

doesn't
make

it
any

less
there

Pieces of me,
omitted for your comfort,
free country,
it once was,
and will be again
but people like you and me,
we've got to stand,
together
for better or worse,
blessing or a curse,
we decide with our words

Your attitude is supposed to protect you,
not place you in positions of
powerlessness

So tired of fighting
to feel something here,
when there's a thousand places
so full of feeling,
I'll wish I wasn't there

Sometimes your pain
is someone else's
and you heal
when they
do

Fire flickers,
cracks and pops,
he can not tell when his breathing stops.
Tears trickle,
makeup flows in streams.
The girl that's in his dreams.
Her voice breaks,
and she hiccups
"Do you still want me?"
Fire lips hit candy ones
everything is multicolored and sweet.
Fingertips trace jaws,
and jaws trace fingertips,
all the while,
love falls into the cracks within their hearts as
the world smiles.
The causes forget to breathe,
and this time he knows he's not dreaming.

I love myself so
no one else has to

The texture painted a different story
one without mercy nor shame
Intricately woven into something
indescribable by words
you had to feel it at
your weakest
moment
to
understand
it's
depth

Her fingers traced
the side of his face
and he tried, hardly
to turn away
but her lips
found his ear
and she whispered
"you made everything here"
he knew
she meant
he made her
exactly the way
he dreamed her

Capabilities unimaginable
by a consciousness of your caliber,
pure talent but you could barely see it,
it's not up to me,
it's all about the way that you choose to
perceive it;

I'm high, dreaming,
past my mind,
scheming,
manifesting things I've been idolizing since I
was a young demon
but now I'm practicing a God's flow,
perfecting my reality based on where my heart
goes
it's hard core this life that we're living in,
and most of y'all ain't even living it;
you're living for the pursuit of possessions,
material obsessions,
only worried about impressing them instead of
yourself;
forgot about the value of character in the
presence of wealth
I know I sound like I'm getting ahead of myself
but lately I've just been feeling like a God in a
bland land:
(continued.)

searching for sanity within a trash can,
in the mind of a madman,
majority oppressed and stretched to their
limits
while the man in the top position
has got a silk tie and his pants are fitted,

it's bullshit, all gimmicks,
lies to distract you,
drugs to relax you,
truths diluted so they could pass through
minds that weren't shaped
to properly contemplate our true fate

but it's never too late to move forward,
we gotta stop focusing on the bad,
we've got to do more good,
we can't spend all of our time being sad,
we've got to do more good
and if there is anything that you heard out of all
the words said
I hope it's that we've got to do more good

(end.)

So many different kinds of love
And we don't
Get to choose
Which one
We feel
For who

Life is bland
if
you
don't
season it

I wonder
And
I wander
In my curious mind
And curious beautiful things
I find
And I wonder while I wander
Amongst all these fellow minds
And wonder do I always why
No one else seems to be as excited as I
To share what others have decidedly
wandered to find
Ponder
and
ponder must I
Questioning things past my met eye
Why these beautiful creations hide
Behind ego's and behavioral issues easily
shattered by
intention put to use
So you see I've been confused
Smart are we
All of us claim to be
But stuck in an undeniable
Monotonous fray
So i must have to say
That you can see
Where my curiousness came to be

(continued.)
You see for me I am intrigued
By who you choose to be

In every moment I will listen if you choose to
share
Because matter we all do please
Admit you realize these little things
We all know
we know

(end.)

When the world outside
Is cold to you
And it will be
It will warm you
To be someone's
Home

Seemingly never ending sky

Hovering over miles and miles of wet pavement

But really it's only my mind

That's wandering

I dream of one day

Taking my feet out for a stroll

Far past the places I think I know

And like you do a dream
         I forgot about you

I burn like fire
Your reaction
Overflowing desire
I never tire
Indefatigable
Cutting like sharp wire
But my reasons are reasonable
Red headed woman
With a fiery demon soul
What are you doing with your life
Is it meaningful

Oh won't you

Be truthful

And honest

Or I'll just break your heart

The hardest

We're all a different shade of the same color

Forest blooded
City slicker
Just trying to understand myself
So i can explain it to you

Maybe I'm not really here

Maybe this is just a dream

Maybe you're not really here

Maybe it's just me

I

AM

SEX

ART

FREEDOM

BORN

WITHIN

THE

BONES

OF

A

HEDON

Love your broken pieces
Before you put yourself back together
You'll fit better

In this small space
Between today and tomorrow
with my eyes closed
I hope I see you

I am not afraid
I am human
I am love
I am radiant
And
Indestructible
I was made by
A god
Far greater than
Any hate
This dream
Can cast
Upon me

Think of all the different turns

We can take within a day

That could take you on roads

You'd never have thought to travel

Sometimes we end up in the greatest places

by accident

And sometimes the worst places

By searching for them

Under the clouds
And over the stream
Into the love
And
Living the dream

Everything
Was
Made
For
Me

No

Rhyme

Or

Reason

Just a burning desire

To

Be

Your

Favorite

Season

Stands out like sugar in the dirt
No purpose
Purely just to sweeten the surface

I
Just want
To
Understand
Let's
Hold hands
Don't
Hurt me

I'm sorry
I ever told you to change
To do something different
Because what I was doing
Was trying to make you
Be somebody else
I'm sorry
When you find that someone
They will love you
Just the way you are
So be you
Do not let anyone
Claiming to 'be the one'
Change you
You are perfect
To someone
It just wasn't me
No matter how hard
We tried to force it
I'm sorry

Sweet lips
And a sour soul
It's a good thing
No one knows
Where your mind goes
When you're alone

When

I was young

I dreamed about a love

Like you

So deep and true

Fear didn't surface

When I first found you

I swore I didn't deserve it

Remember
To
Take
Yourself
Off
Of
Autopilot
Show
The
World
Your
Layers

Every inch of her,

Even the immeasurable

Essence on the inside,

Absolutely mesmerizing

All of her,

Down to the little

Raised spots on her legs,

That I secretly wished

One day she'd let me

Trace with my fingertips

Or better yet,

My lips

There isn't a specific trait that makes a woman
captivating.
It lies within the simple fact that she knows.
She
knows her power and that's
what captures
You.

You
don't have
to
build her up,
she built herself.

Create so much comfort that it
inspires growth,
not
requires it

Forever thankful for

The what seemed to be

Tiny inconveniences that

Always end up leading me

Onto greater things

Than I have ever dreamed

There are things
I feel when
I'm with you
That make me
Forget
Other people
Exist

Please,
Don't get so consumed
With your big leaps
That you forget about
The small steps that
Lead you to those
Revolutionary moments

I prefer to live in the spaces
that make my heart race

Flowers in the field
Rocking like the ocean
In the breeze,
Kisses as soft as the
Feathers of the bird,
Sitting so high up in the tree's;
Singing a song to
It's lover.

Dear,
Sing a song to me.

No one could ever

Take your place

But someone else fits better

In the space

I tried to fill with you

Shining
In the
Sunlight
Like the
Goddess
That I am
growing
A garden
From my
Heart
Where
Is it
That you
Stand

He was there that night
Between us
And I knew
Before I found you
That i'd lost you
Yet I kept searching
Anyway

At times I stray
From the words on the pages
To write words
On pages
Of my own

Twisted
Beliefs
Because
Desire
Is
All
That
Is
True

Time passed
And here we are
Not far from where
We started
But so much closer
To where we're going
A past filled with
So many people
And yet so busy
Being lonely
Finally
With you
I get to be
Home

Free

Ripped to shreds
Torn from the seams
And yet it seems
That
I'm scared
To be left
Holding nothing
Even if it's shambles
At least i'm not
Alone
Terrifying
Yes
I know
I've got to let
My demons
Go

Do not deprive yourself of life
Learn how to do more than survive
Thrive

We loved to think
That they lived
In misery
But truly
That was
Just you
And me

What if

This life

Is everything

You ever wanted

But you fought it

Everytime you got it

Manifest destiny

But you're busy

Fighting with the

Recipe

You are
A story

Flawlessly
Written

By an
Author

Too
Perfect

For a
Name

And through the reeds
They heard the words
That changed their worlds
Forever
They knew right then
That they were the words
That wrote this world
To be together
Most things since changed
But some remain
Of lavender
Leaves
And eyes of green
A fate I had hoped
You won't know

Not all things
Get better
With time

Some things
Still hurt
When you
Look at
Them

Some times
Life is
About
Finding something
Better to
Look at
Than your pain

I saw
what an unlived life
looked like
and so I choose to live mine

Opportunity

Left on the floor
Like you don't remember me

Blame

Instead of me
You carry

Confused
Is what I am

I looked for you
And found myself

My calls to you
Fell on deaf ears

Years of time
That now weigh nothing

I blame you
You blame me

We're both wrong

Arms crossed
eyes on me
I didnt think
I'd change
a thing
the
honesty
cut deep
salt water
on my cheeks
you went
after me
snowflakes
fell and
I told you
my truth
the rest is
our
history

She couldn't tell you what it was
maybe the sunset
or the way her skates slid across the ground
she loved fresh pavement
her heart was racing
maybe it was something in the air
in the trees
could of been the time of year
or maybe it was him
it was always him
as she skated closer
she knew she wasn't going back
they'd leave tonight
because going back wasn't an option
they were here now
and forward they would go

Follow you down
to the end of the road
where the sidewalk ends
and the grass won't grow
there's just dirt here
dry and warm
no one's home
they've all moved on
we're alone now
it's the same old song
we were young once
but that times gone
I thought i'd miss them
but it's been so long
nothing left
and yet
no regrets

No real attempt
at defense
weaker than wet cardboard
conscience heavy
guilt ridden
so many things
I tried to run from
you were always there though
the minute that my eyes closed
I never really got away

Everyday
the screws in my cage
loosen
the god I have bound
gets more and more
restless
these bonds I will burn

I was fearful
I held myself prisoner
primitive concepts
of self
holding me hostage
I let it all go
I am
free